CHRONICLE BOOKS

ON FLOWERS

Book of Days

BY

Kathryn Kleinman and Sara Slavin

Calligraphy courtesy
of Alan Hutchison
Publishing Co. Ltd.

ISBN: 0-87701-656-9

Printed in Japan
by Dai Nippon Printing
Co., Ltd., Tokyo.

Distributed in Canada
by Raincoast Books
112 East 3rd Avenue
Vancouver, B.C. V5T1C8

10 9 8 7 6 5 4 3 2 1

Chronicle Books
275 Fifth Street
San Francisco, CA 94103

PHOTOGRAPHY

Kathryn Kleinman

STYLING

Sara Slavin

TEXT

Linda Peterson

DESIGN

Michael Mabry

FOOD

Amy Nathan

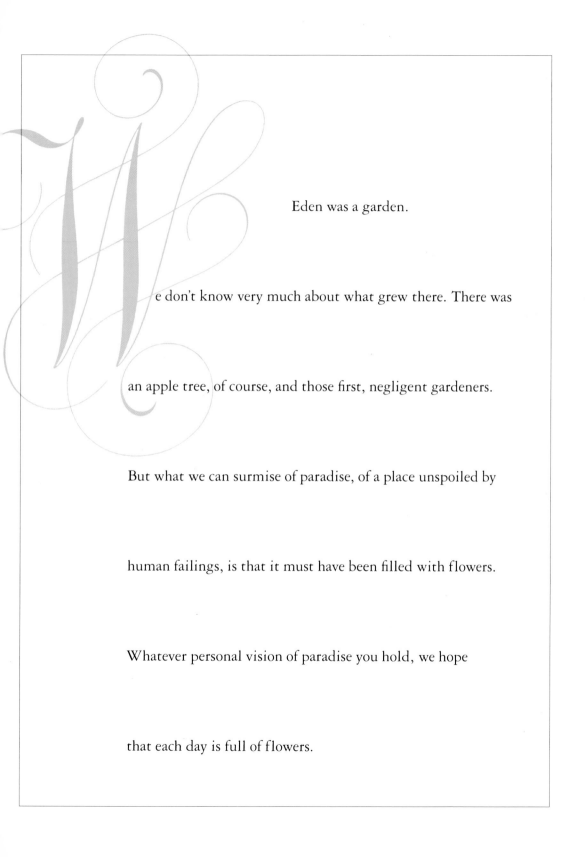

Eden was a garden.

We don't know very much about what grew there. There was

an apple tree, of course, and those first, negligent gardeners.

But what we can surmise of paradise, of a place unspoiled by

human failings, is that it must have been filled with flowers.

Whatever personal vision of paradise you hold, we hope

that each day is full of flowers.

January

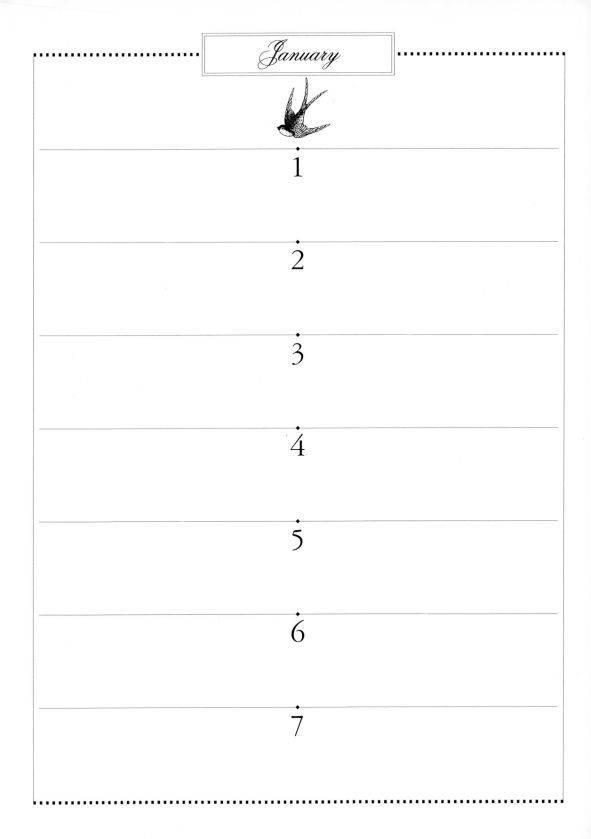

1

2

3

4

5

6

7

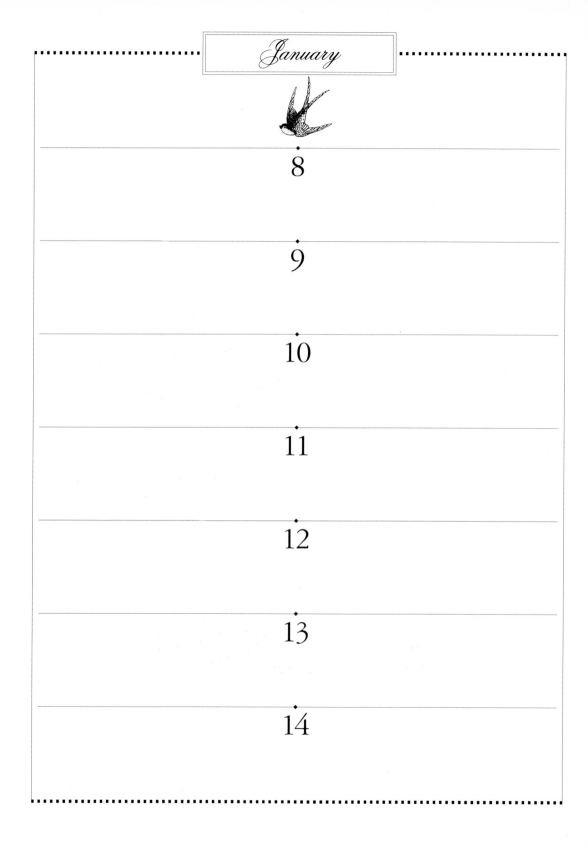

8

9

10

11

12

13

14

January

15

16

17

18

19

20

21

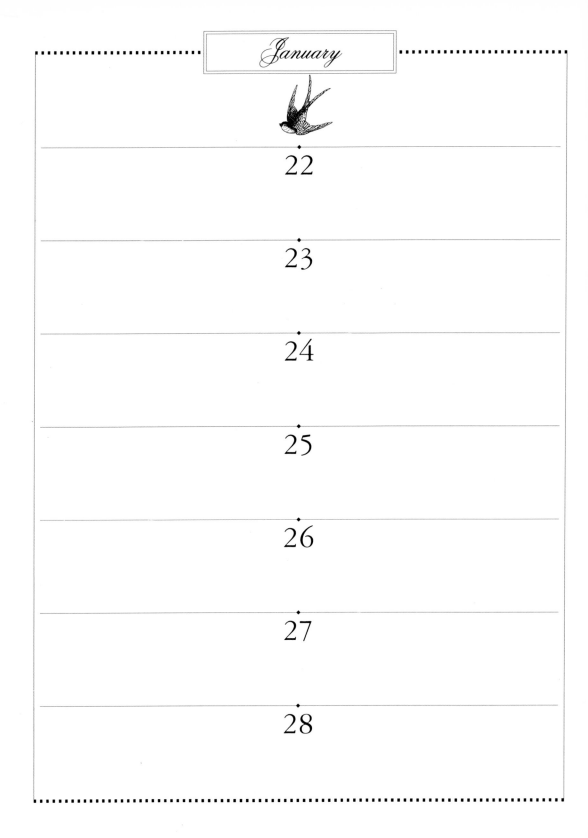

January

22

23

24

25

26

27

28

H istory is
unclear on the subject of gift
giving. There were the three Wise
Men, of course, with gold,
frankincense, and myrrh. There
were the Greeks and that
untrustworthy gift horse. There were
Native Americans shower-
ing neighbors with potlatch gifts,
designed to show off their
wealth. But the sweetest gifts
deliver their sentiments
before they are even opened.

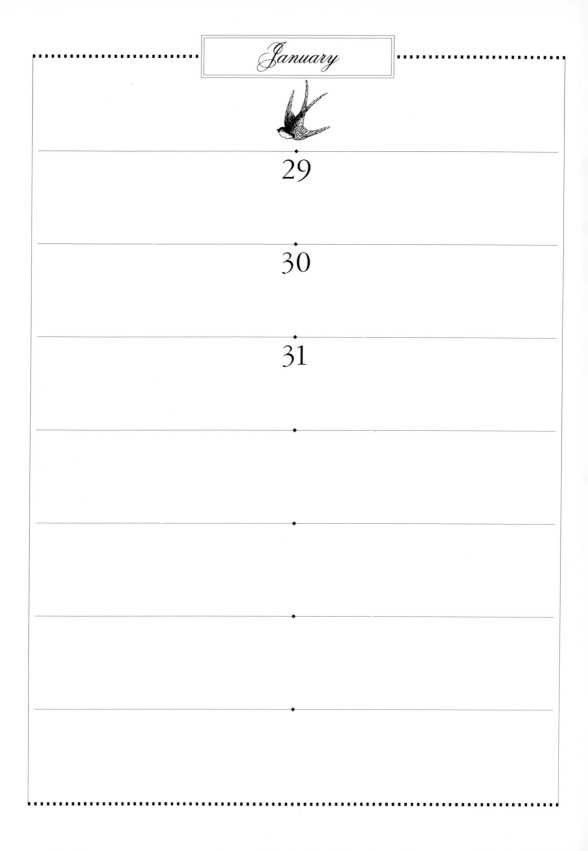

January

29

30

31

"All my hurts/My garden spade can heal,"

wrote Emerson in *Musketaquid*. Herbalists, homeopaths,

poets and romantics are right: Flowers may

not cure everything, but they can spin a powerful spell.

February

1

2

3

4

5

6

7

8

9

10

11

12

13

14

In the 1890s,
the word corsage changed its
meaning. Originally
a corsage referred to the bodice
of a woman's dress, but
just before the turn of the century,
the word came to mean
a small bouquet, worn as an
ornament.

15

16

17

18

19

20

21

Flower lovers are inveterate fact gatherers: Dissolve a little Epsom salts in the water (1 tsp. salts to 1 quart water) when you bring your watering can around the geraniums, and they will bloom prolifically. Or force a rosebud open early by choosing buds that feel a bit soft to the touch, then blow hard into the top of the bud. Or bury nails in the ground around your blue hydrangeas, and their color will deepen. ¶ Sound principles of botany are involved in most of these old wives' tales. Even flower arranging includes principles of aesthetics, made to be followed, and broken. Some flower arrangers employ what is called the Hogarth Curve. William Hogarth (1697–1764), an English painter and engraver, saw beauty in curves rather than geometric shapes. In 1745, he painted a self-portrait posed beside his dog, Trump. The painting hangs in the Tate Gallery in London, and if you visit it, you'll see a palette in the painting, inscribed with a lazy, serpentine line and the words, "line of beauty." ¶ Later, in his *Analysis of Beauty,* Hogarth explained that he considered this curve the most perfect figure humans could devise. In classic flower arrangements it has become a guideline for creating pleasing shapes. ¶ A love for variations frees you to consider the curve and then abandon it, or to create your own curve simply by gathering flowers in every tone of pink, purple, and cream and tying them up with ribbon.

22

23

24

25

26

27

28/29

March

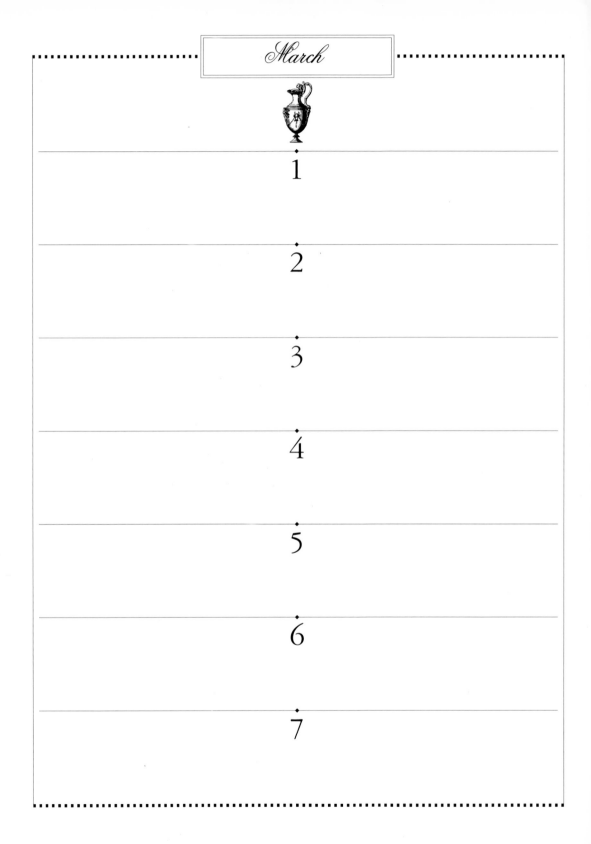

1

2

3

4

5

6

7

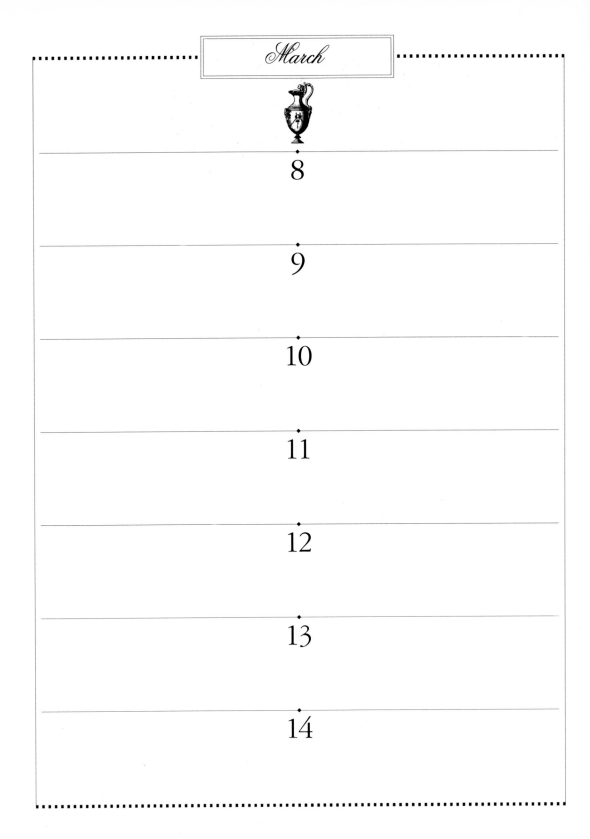

8

9

10

11

12

13

14

The art of

containing flowers

is as much

an art of subtraction

as it is

of addition.

March

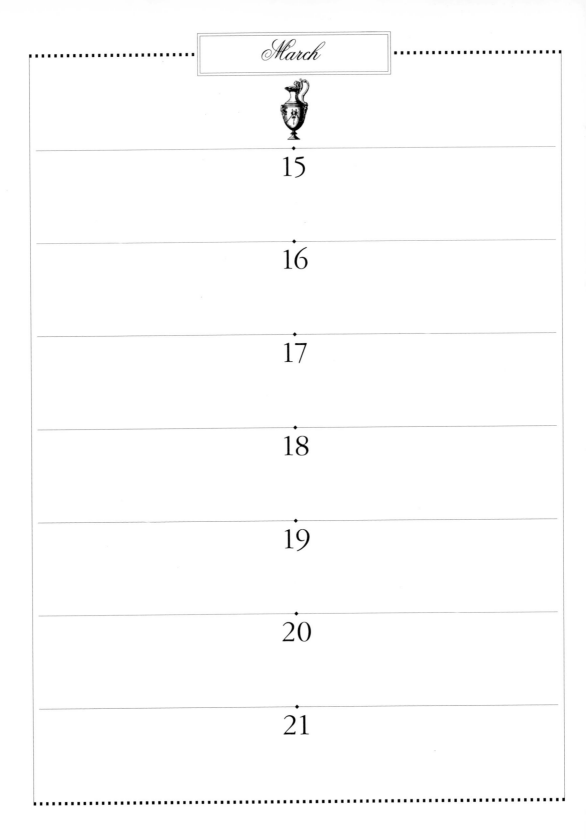

15

16

17

18

19

20

21

Sweet apple whites
Drift through springtime sky.
Adam falls again.

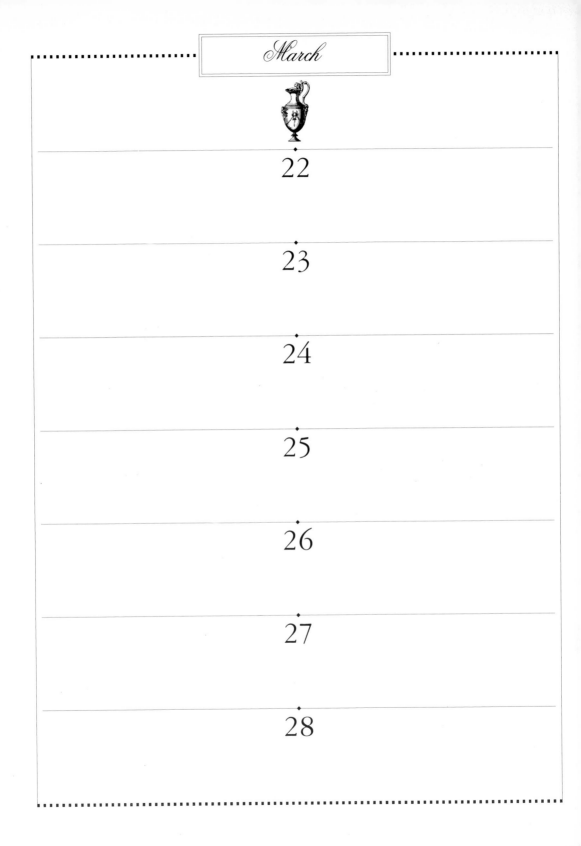

22

23

24

25

26

27

28

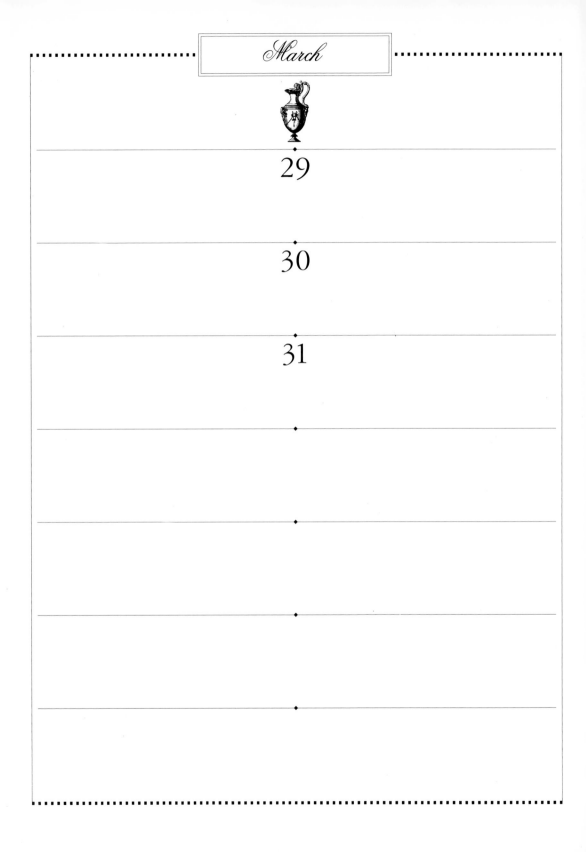

29

30

31

The essence of flowers is that they are both symbols and tangible,

sweet-smelling markers for all the occasions, great and small in life.

April

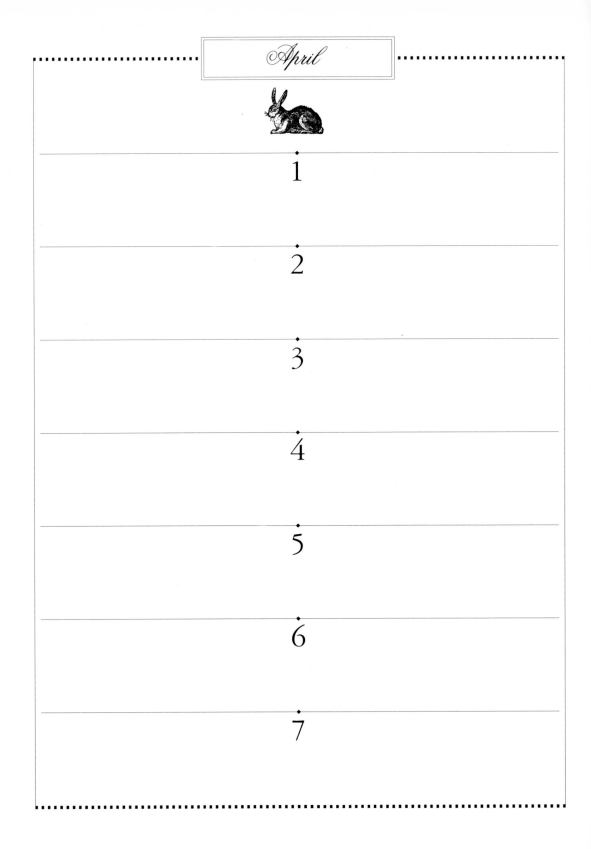

1

2

3

4

5

6

7

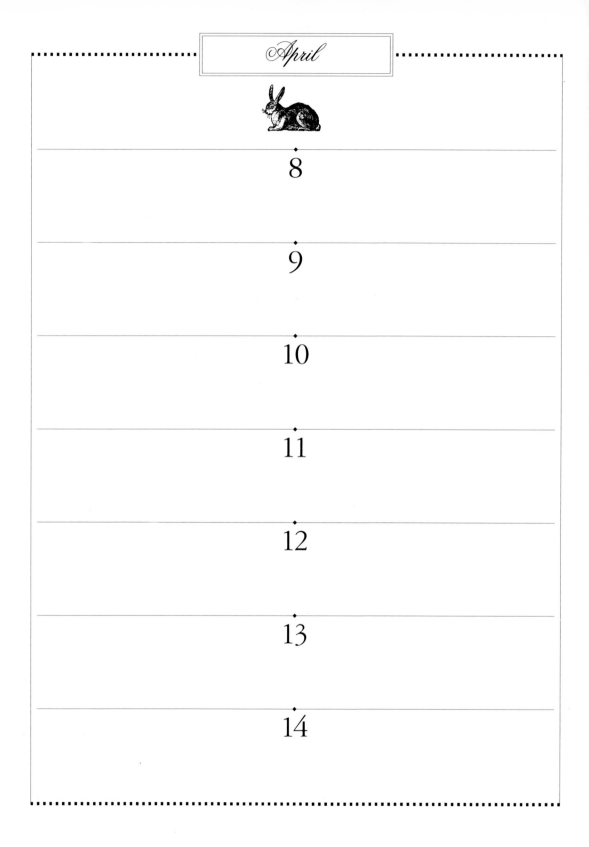

8

9

10

11

12

13

14

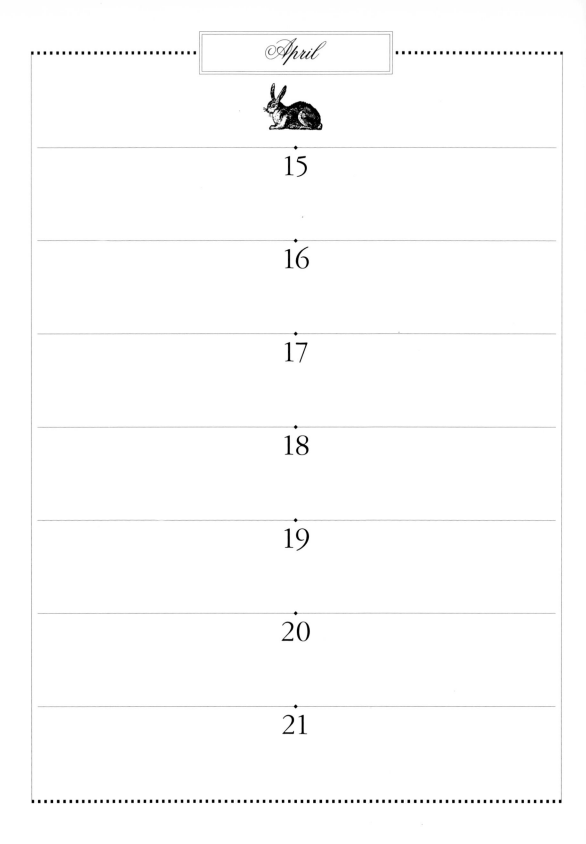

15

16

17

18

19

20

21

From "Mary, Mary,
Quite Contrary" to "Daffy-
down-dilly," some
favorite Mother Goose rhymes
have chronicled the
relationship between children
and flowers.

April

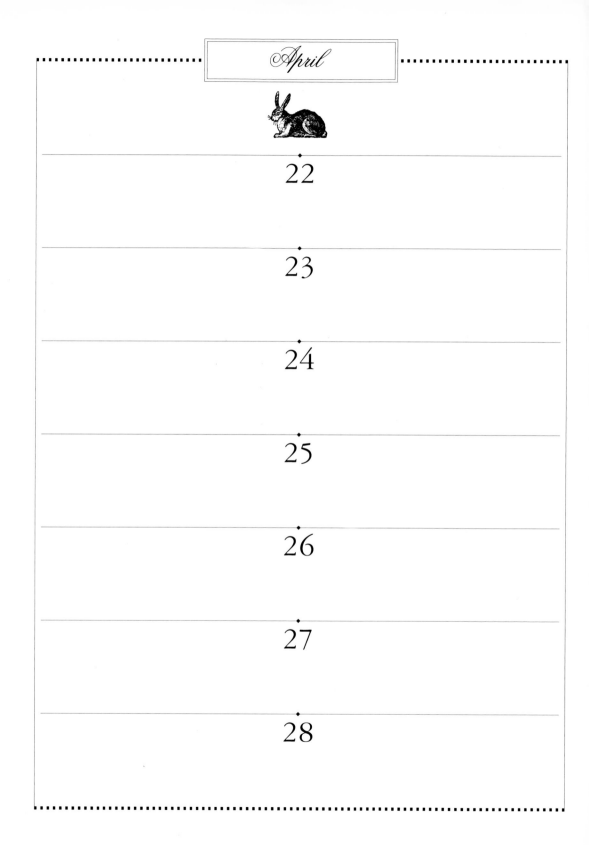

22

23

24

25

26

27

28

29

30

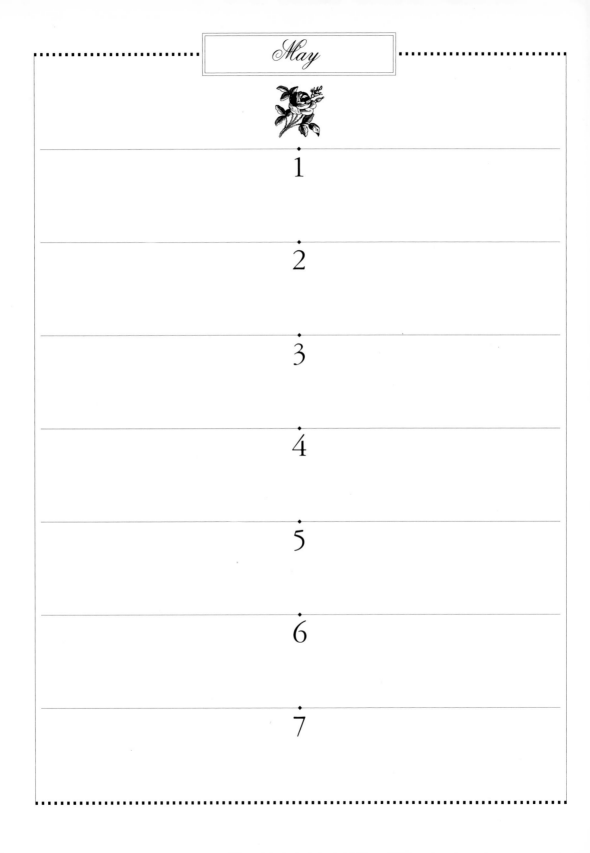

May

1

2

3

4

5

6

7

A Chinese fairy tale tells of the gardens of the Western Queen Mother in the land of perpetual bloom. It is the story of the peach thief who promises the governor and everyone in the town square that he can produce any fruit in any season.

The governor asks for a peach. From a bamboo box, the peach thief pulls a coil of rope, hundreds of feet long, and throws it into the heavens. It stays there, as if suspended from the sky. As the crowd watches, the peach thief sends his young son, climbing, climbing into the heavens. The boy disappears into the clouds. The father waits, then suddenly a peach falls to earth. The peach thief presents it to the governor.

A cheer goes up, but it turns to gasps when moments later the son himself falls to earth— in pieces. The old peach thief sadly packs the pieces of his son away in the bamboo box. Shocked and heartbroken, the crowd presses funeral donations upon him. He accepts the gifts gratefully, tucks them away, and then knocks on his bamboo box. "You can come out now, my son," he says, "and thank the generous donors." The box flies open and out jumps the son, sound of body and wreathed in smiles.

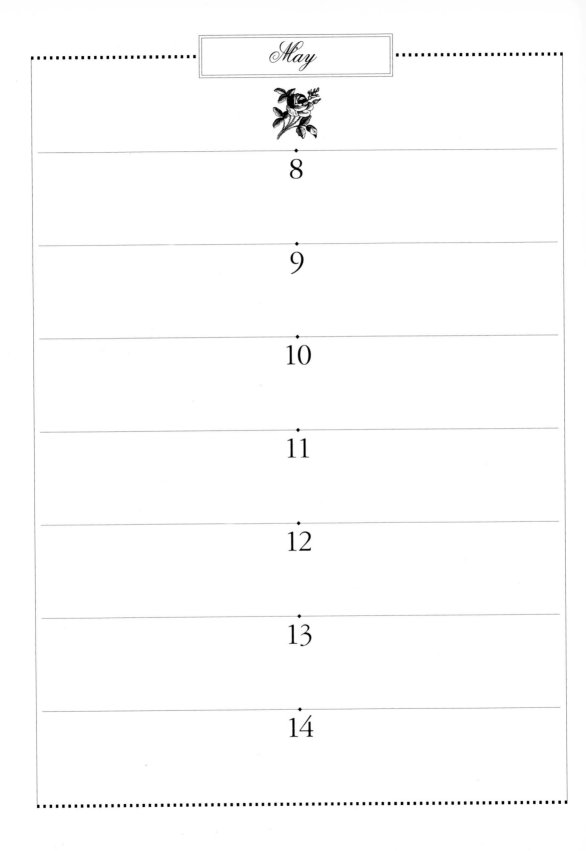

May

8

9

10

11

12

13

14

Vichyssoise with Violets

Ingredients

2 shallots, sliced

5 leeks, white and pale green portions, sliced thin

2 tablespoons unsalted butter

4 medium potatoes, peeled and sliced thin

¼ cup dry white wine

5 cups chicken broth

1 cup half & half

Dash salt

Dash white pepper

Cucumber, sliced for garnish

Violets for garnish

Method

In a large saucepan sauté shallots and leeks in the butter over low heat for 10 minutes. Add potatoes, wine and broth. Bring to a boil. Reduce to simmer. Cover and cook 25 minutes. Process in small batches in a food processor until smooth. Add half and half. Salt and pepper to taste and mix well. Chill. Serve cold in individual soup bowls. Garnish with various cucumber shapes. Float a violet on each serving.

Yield: 8 servings.

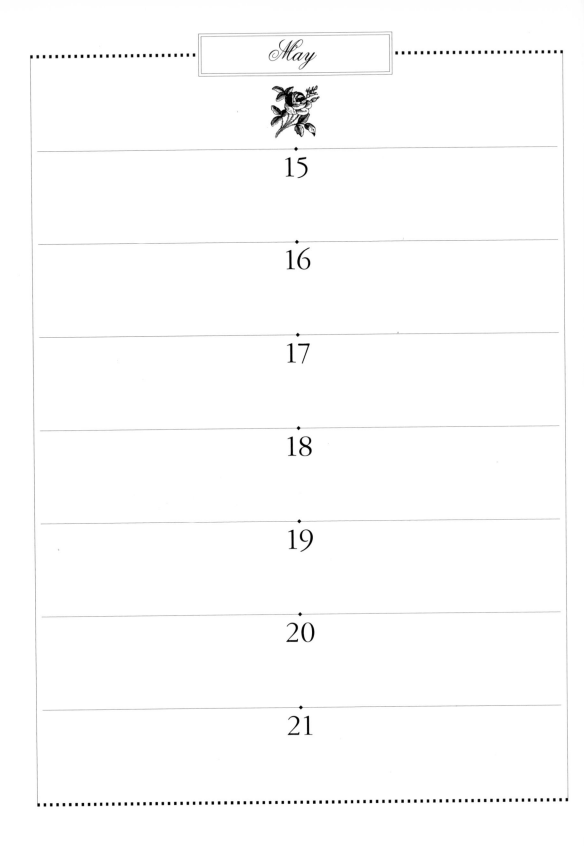

15

16

17

18

19

20

21

*Violets figure in stories from
mythology to George Bernard Shaw. You may
remember that Eliza Doolittle sold
violets before she became a lady and learned to
pronounce her "h's." But did you know
that Venus herself turned white violets blue?
She did it for spite when her son
Cupid admired the white blooms for their
purity and sweetness.*

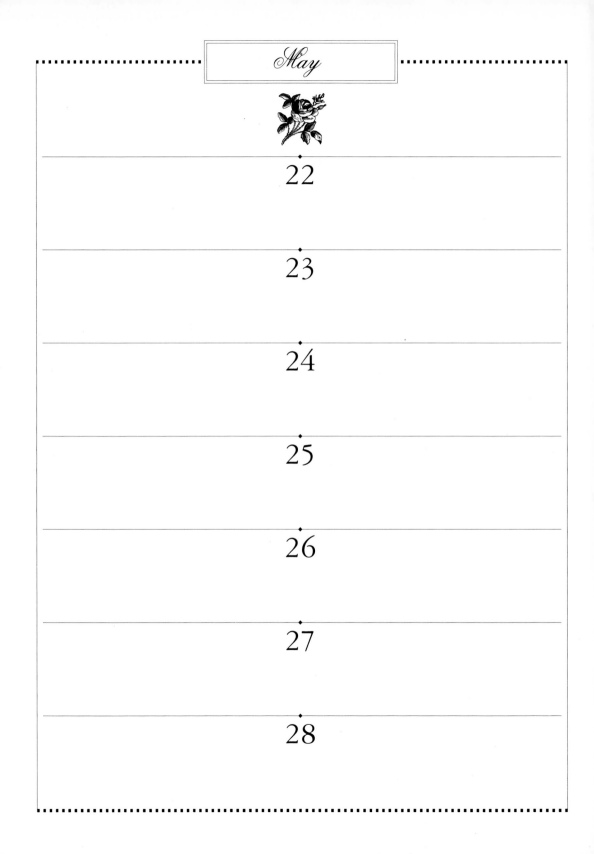

May

22

23

24

25

26

27

28

May

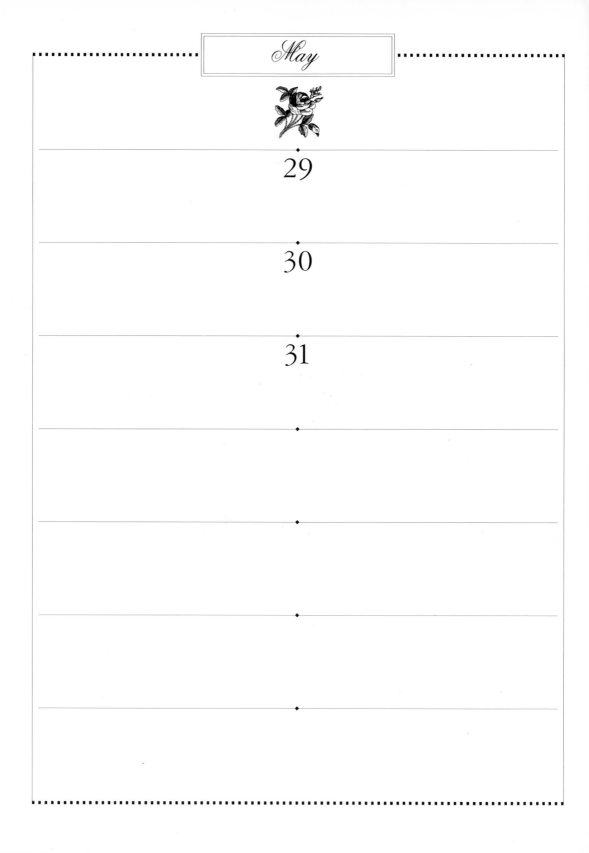

29

30

31

Flowers have faces as distinctive and individual as people.

The French believed that the pansy had a pensive or thoughtful face and dubbed it

herbe de la pensée, the flower of thought or remembrance.

English gardeners took up the word pensée and Anglicized the spelling to pansy.

June

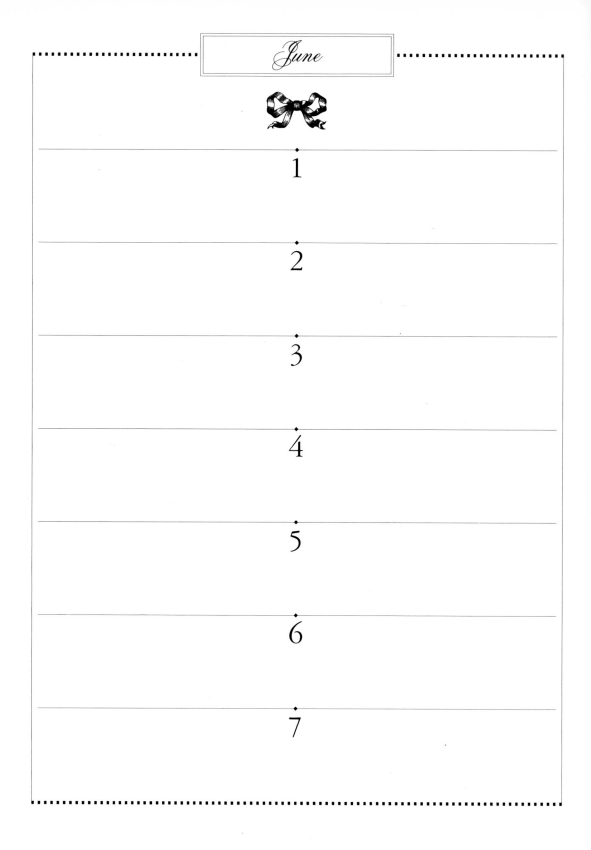

1

2

3

4

5

6

7

Cleopatra carpeted the floor with fresh roses for Mark Anthony.

Our bed dreams down the Nile

Under bright summer roses I cultivated for you.

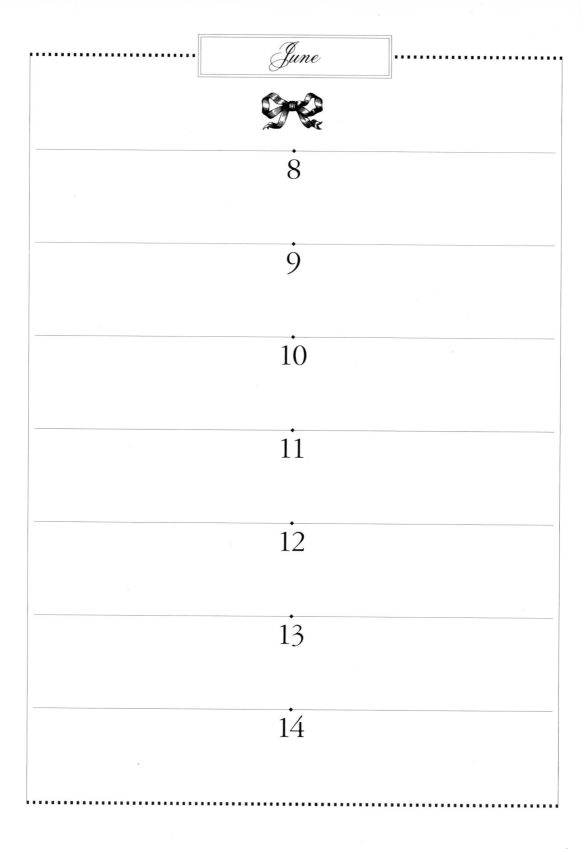

June

8

9

10

11

12

13

14

William Shakespeare knew that when words fail, flowers work. In *A Midsummer Night's Dream,* Oberon sends Puck, armed only with pansies, to make mischief with Titania. Though we may think of pansies as friendly, even ordinary, Shakespeare knew better. He reminds us the pansy's country name is "love-in-idleness." Says Oberon to Puck, "Fetch me that flower; the herb I show'd thee once: /The juice of it on sleeping eyelids laid/Will make a man or woman madly dote/Upon the next live creature that it sees." Love-in-idleness works, at least in Puck's naughty hands, and poor Titania falls hopelessly, helplessly in love with a man wearing a donkey's head.

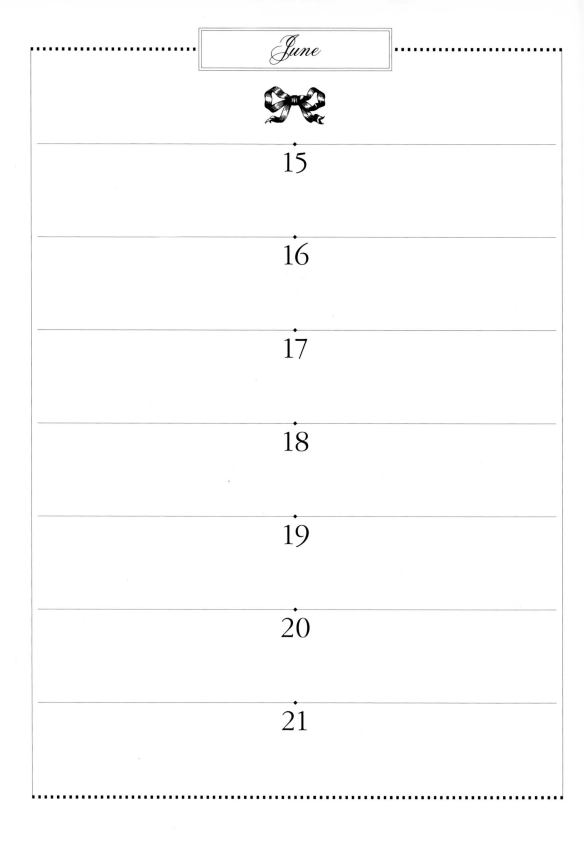

June

15

16

17

18

19

20

21

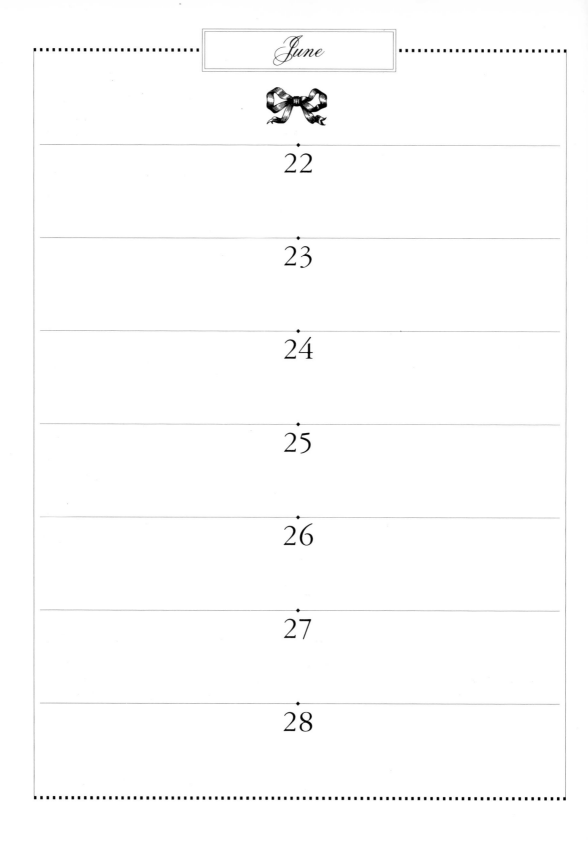

June

22

23

24

25

26

27

28

29

30

July

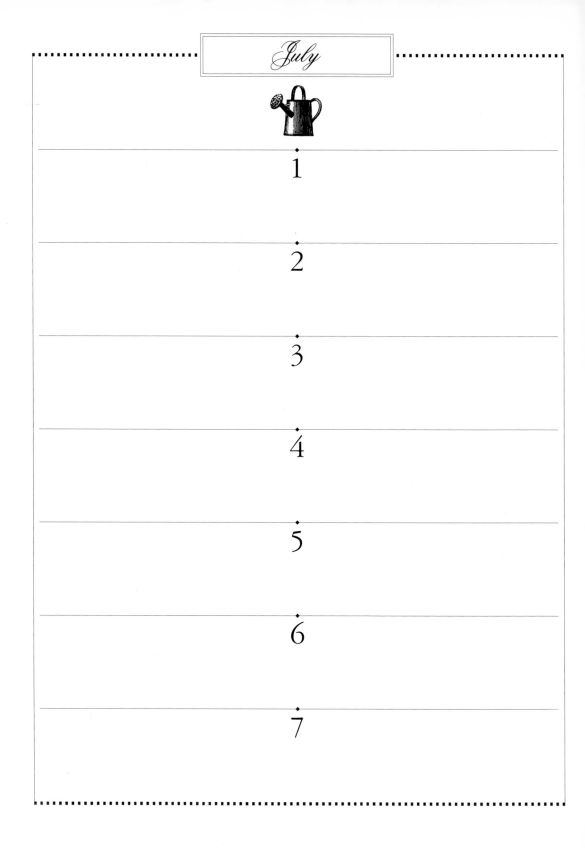

1

2

3

4

5

6

7

It is magic, I tell him,
Nena's magic. Her grace
with all things green and
growing.
There must be special secrets
in my mother's garden.

Everything grows in
my mother's garden:
Camellias, delicate pinks
and whites, splendid scarlets,
Graceful lilies, regal iris,
cheerful ranunculus.

All of us, family and friends,
We marvel at my mother's
garden,
She must know secrets,
we think.

Good things to eat grow in
my mother's garden.
Tomatoes as sweet as fruit,
peppers red and green,
Carrots, sugar peas, baby
lettuce.

And, she does—
Secrets of generosity,
kindness, compassion,
Of life lived honestly,
imaginatively, well.

But now, a mother myself,
I crave a secret or two.
I want to garden, as she does
With grace and love
and skill.

'Coleslaw grows in my
Nena's garden.
That's what my son brags
to his friends.
A city child, he thinks magic
transforms garden treats into
his favorite dish.

Still trim in gardening
clothes,
She brushes dirt and leaves
from her hands
And comes to greet us.

We ordered bulbs together
this summer. She claims to
envy me my tulips. And I?
I want only this,
My son to say one day:

There's much I wish I learned
from my mother:
French seams,
Southern chicken, patience,
painting, some medicine.
For these things I have
no aptitude.

Everything grows in my
mother's garden.

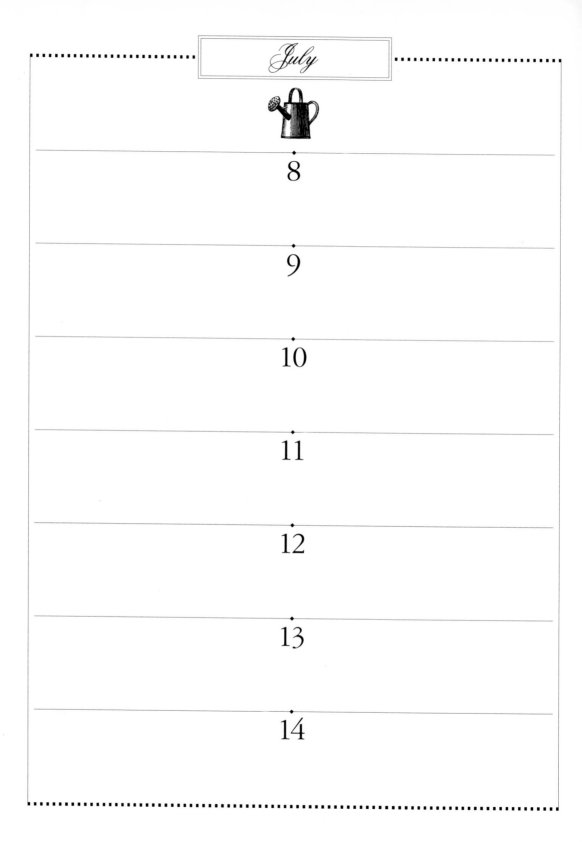

8

9

10

11

12

13

14

Flowers are magic.
The English wove garlands
of St. Johnswort,
sure protection against the
Devil himself.
Those who wore the garlands or
looked through them
at the midsummer bonfire
would be spared
headaches for the year.

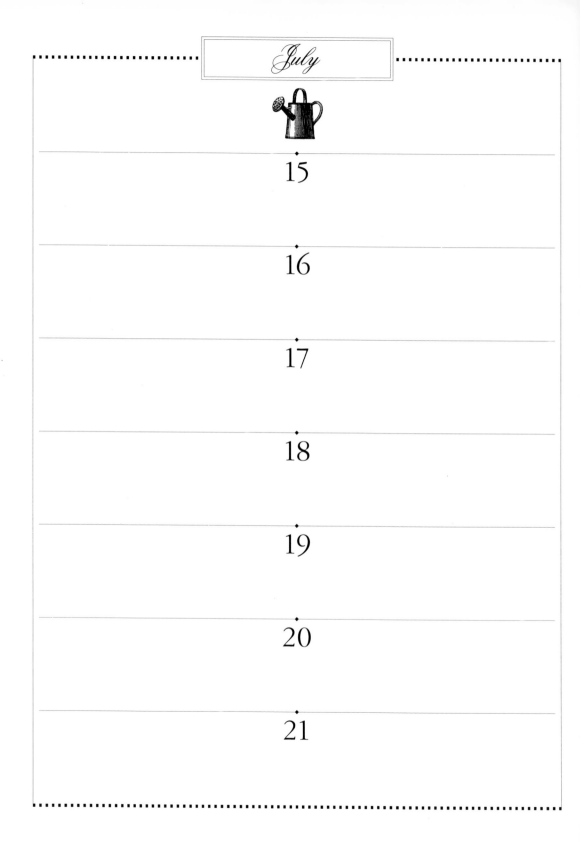

15

16

17

18

19

20

21

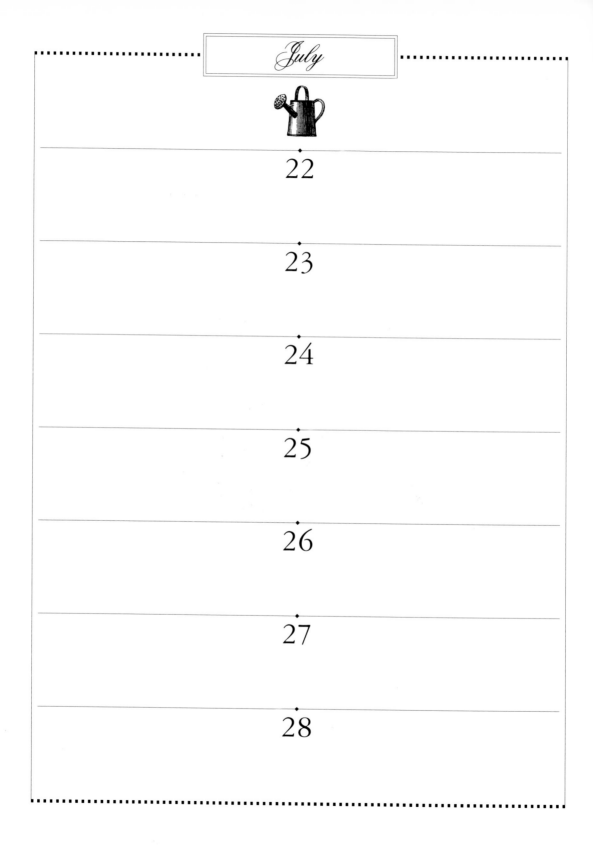

22

23

24

25

26

27

28

MAGNOLIA

HYDRANGEA

SWEET PEA

CALLA LILY

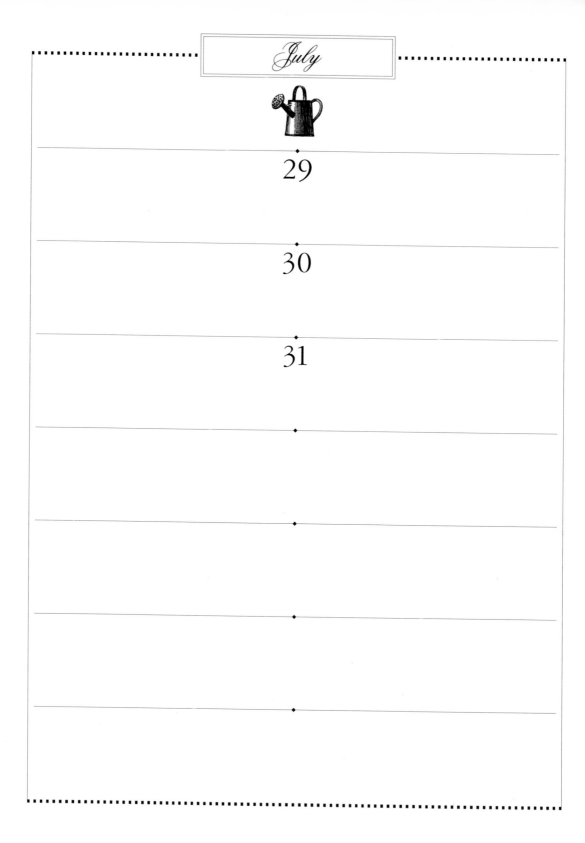

29

30

31

Autumn Delight

August

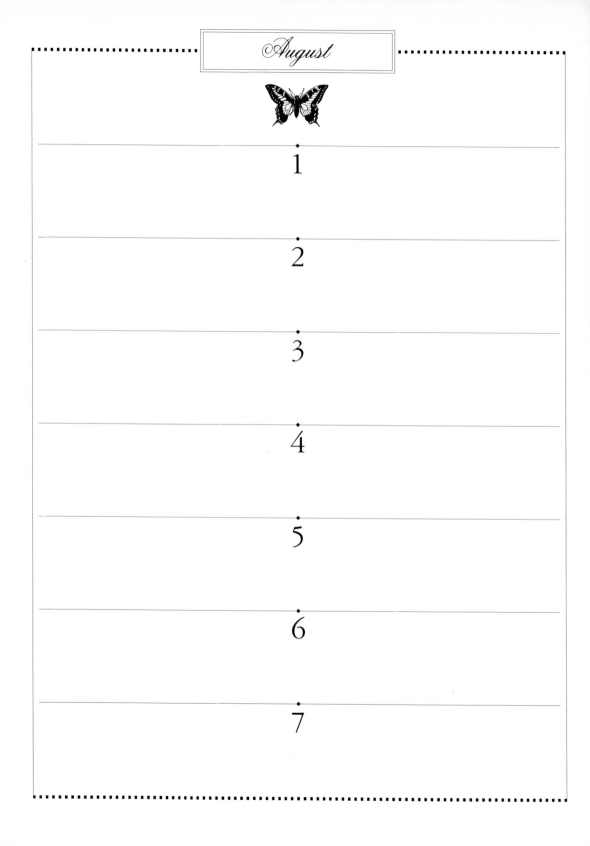

1

2

3

4

5

6

7

8

9

10

11

12

13

14

For the initiated, flowers can offer more than a visual feast; they can please the palate as well. This, we think, was Nature's intent. Unless they are tainted by pesticides or chemical fertilizers, many green and growing things on the earth are good to eat. There's the spicy taste of nasturtiums, the sweet oniony bite of chive blossoms, and the surprising cauliflower notes of chrysanthemum. Good cooks are accustomed to reaching for herbs and spices, but creative cooks know that the flowers, as well as the leaves, add taste and beauty to food. Ignore the little glass bottles on your market shelf and look to the garden instead. Look for tiny snowy white flowers on savory stems, for sky blue rosemary blossoms, for the white or yellow flowers of mustard.

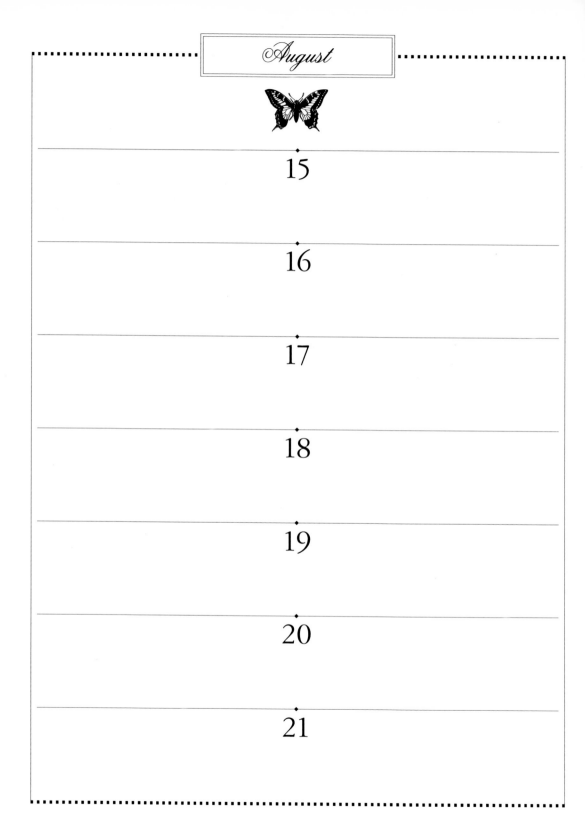

15

16

17

18

19

20

21

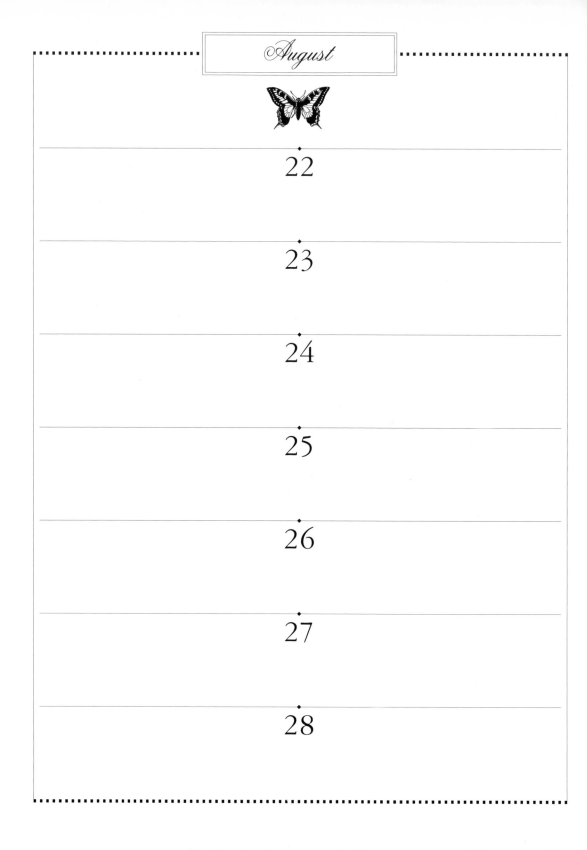

August

22

23

24

25

26

27

28

August

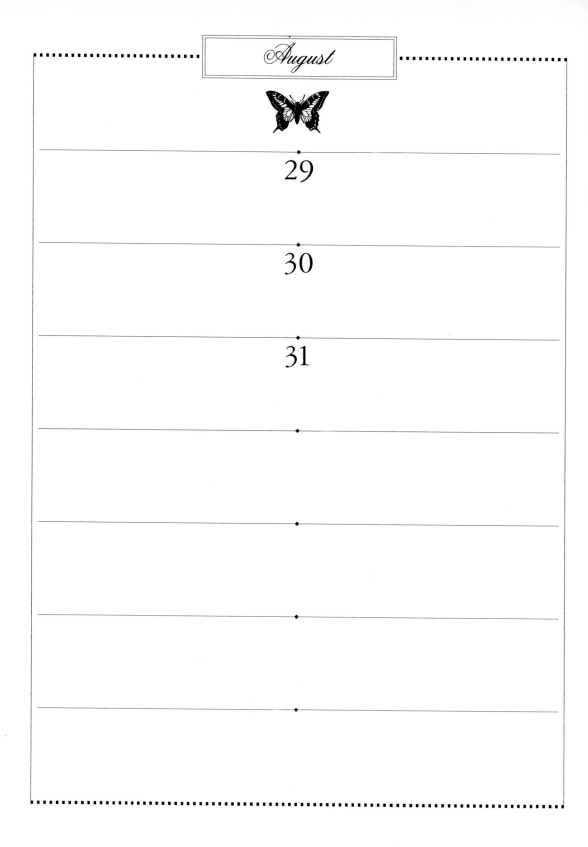

29

30

31

September

1

2

3

4

5

6

7

In Victorian
England, the language of love
was flowers. Lady Wortley
Montague noted that lovers could
send their missives back and
forth, telling volumes, "without
ever inking the fingers."

8

9

10

11

12

13

14

15

16

17

18

19

20

21

"Traume sind Schaume" (Dreams
are froth), wrote Sigmund Freud. That was
a common nineteenth-century
belief until the Viennese master himself
worked to persuade others that
there was much to learn by studying
what he called the Kingdom of
the Illogical. Flowers grow wild and free
in dreams; they have a place of
honor in the Kingdom of the Illogical.

22

23

24

25

26

27

28

29

30

October

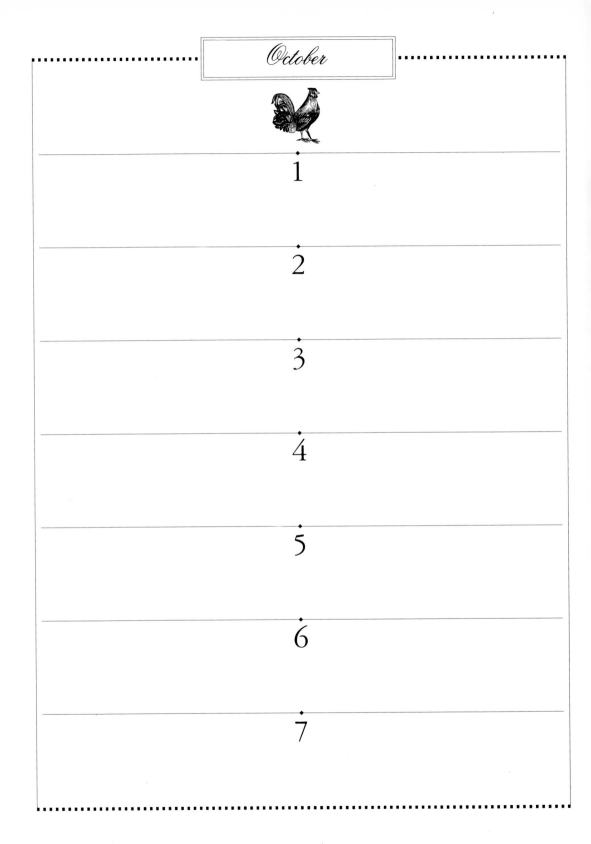

1

2

3

4

5

6

7

Tulips probably first came to England from Turkey

through Vienna during the reign of Queen Elizabeth I. They were

extravagantly expensive, even into the nineteenth

century, putting them out of reach of most amateur gardeners.

8

9

10

11

12

13

14

Nasturtium Pizza

Ingredients

For a 10 to 11-inch pizza:

1   Packaged pizza crust mix
¼ teaspoon blended Italian herbs
2   small or 1 large leek, cleaned,
    sliced thin, and sautéed in
    Rosemary infused olive oil
½ small zucchini
½ small pattypan squash
½ small sunburst squash
3   ounces dry Monterey Jack cheese
½ ounce grated Parmesan cheese
    Handful nasturtium
    petals and blossoms

Method

*Prepare pizza crust as per package
directions for a 12-inch thin-
crust pizza, adding the Italian herbs
to the dry mixture. Shape dough
into a freeform round, 10-11 inches.
Bake on a parchment-lined bak-
ing sheet at 425 degrees on lowest
oven rack for 10 minutes.*

*Slice squashes very thin. Slice cheese
using a cheese plane. Top pizza
crust with leeks and the sliced Jack
cheese and squashes. Bake another
5 to 7 minutes, until cheese melts.
Sprinkle with Parmesan and bake a
few more minutes, until cheese
melts. Sprinkle with nasturtiums.*

Yield: 1 to 2 servings.

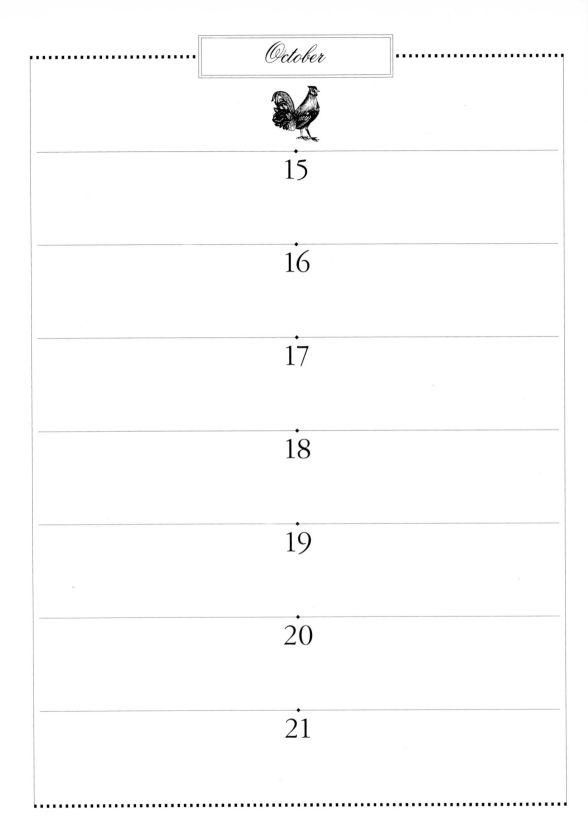

15

16

17

18

19

20

21

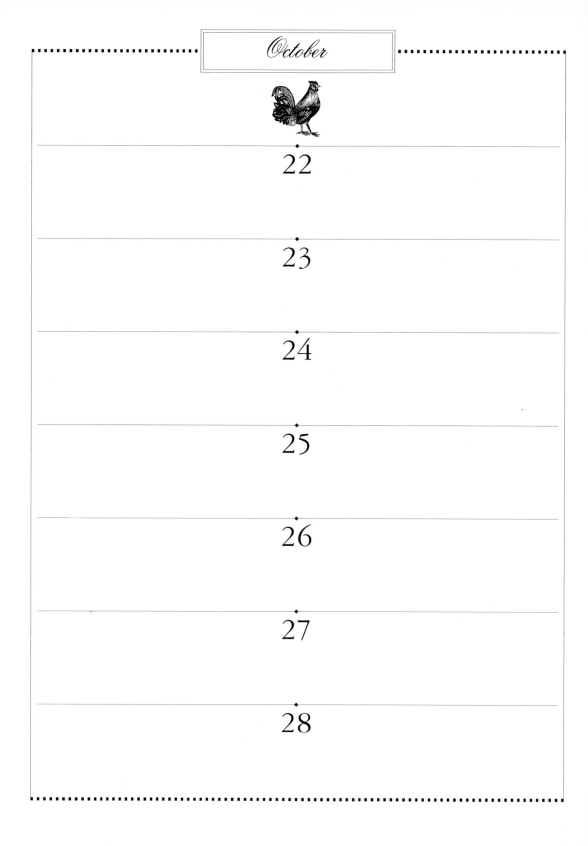

22

23

24

25

26

27

28

Nature provides a garden

pharmacopoeia for insomniacs. Anise,

dill in hot milk, ginseng,

mandrake, marjoram, peppermint,

primrose, and pillows stuffed

with wormwood are all country cures

for insomnia.

29

30

31

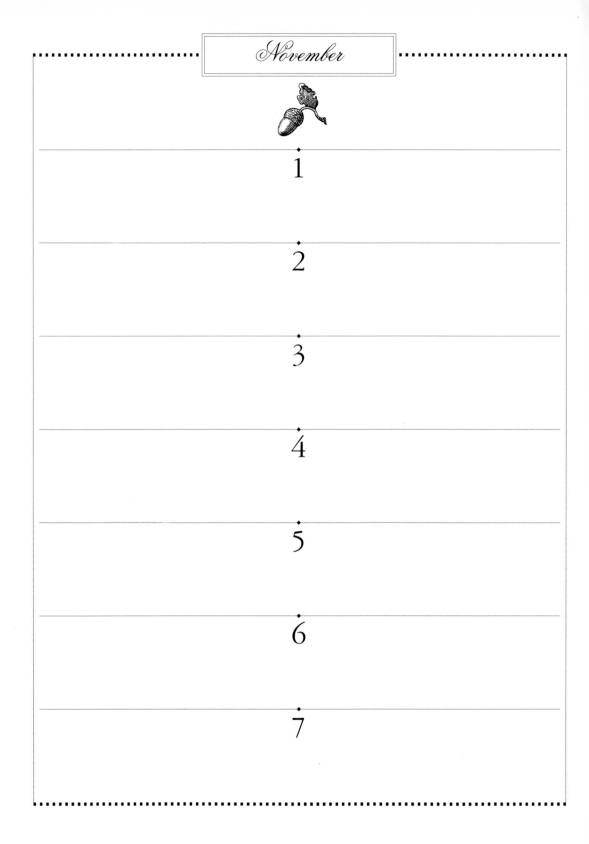

1

2

3

4

5

6

7

Orchids seem the ultimate ornamental flower. They grow in rare

and exotic places, in inaccessible corners of the tropics, in hothouses, in trees, on mountains at

altitudes up to 14,000 feet. Unless Nature does the growing, orchids can require great care and

patience; some species take from five to ten years to develop from seed to flower. Orchids have their

practical side as well, the genus Vanilla yields seeds that are fermented into cooking vanilla.

8

9

10

11

12

13

14

November

15

16

17

18

19

20

21

Hand-tied bouquets. Potpourri.

Perfumes. Attars. Wreaths. Remedies. The true

flower lover is never limited

by so pedestrian a concept as the vase.

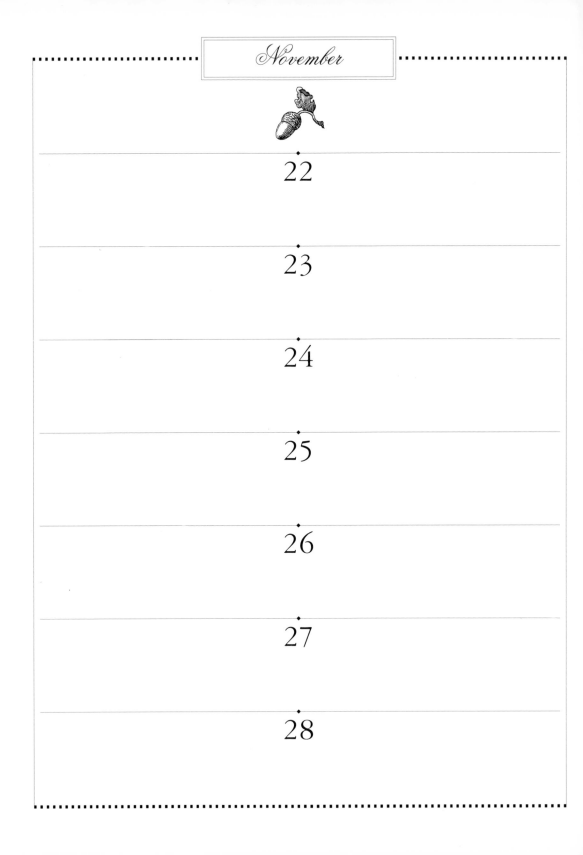

22

23

24

25

26

27

28

29

30

December

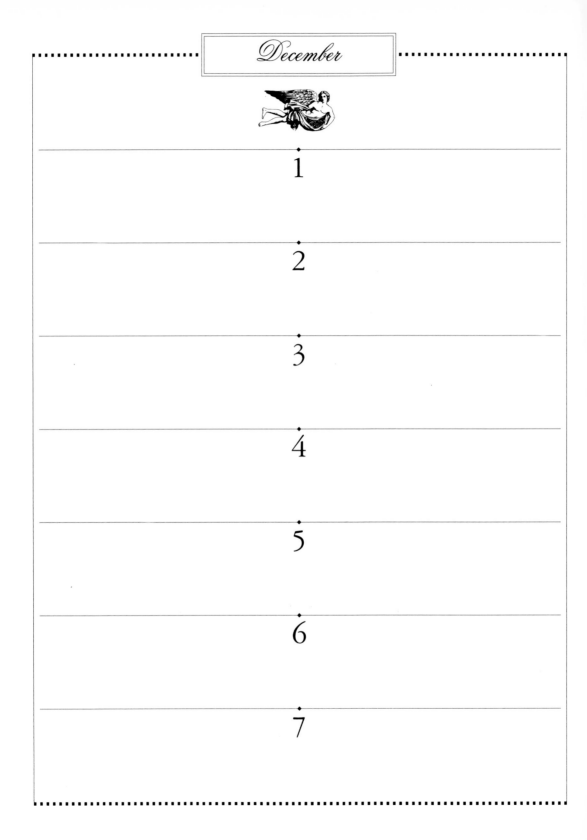

1

2

3

4

5

6

7

There was
the Black Dahlia, a puzzling
murder that rocked Los
Angeles in the 1930s. And then
there was Brenda Starr's
mysterious sweetheart, the man
in the eyepatch who left
black orchids on the pillow when
he came to call. Finally,
we developed a dozen midnight
roses—smoky images
that arrived almost of their
own accord.

December

8

9

10

11

12

13

14

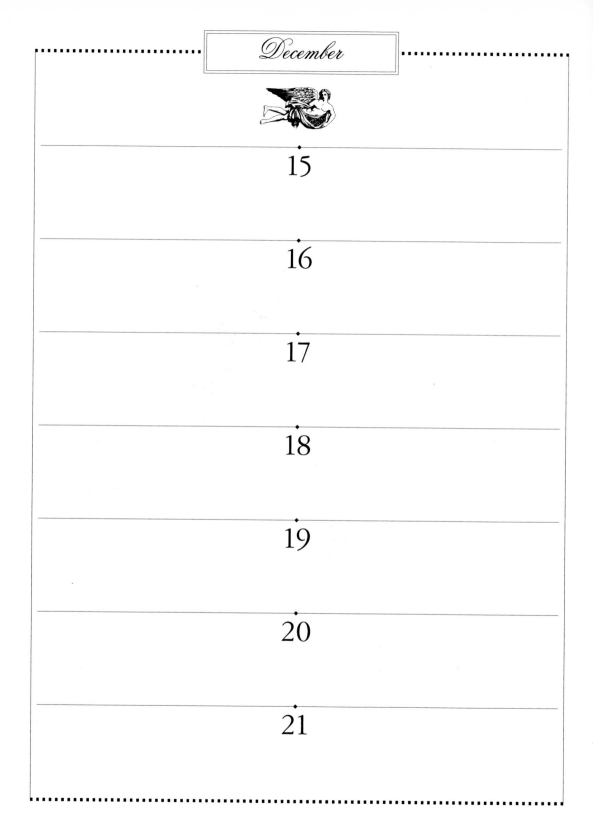

December

15

16

17

18

19

20

21

Of the many stories about St. Nicholas, the fourth-century prelate who became the patron saint of Russia, sailors, and children, the old stories are best, and the most beautiful. It seems that once upon a time, the good bishop heard about a town far away where people went hungry, even the children. He asked his servants to bring him "the fruits of your gardens and the fruits of your fields," to feed those far-off children. His servants were kind and generous people, so they gathered great baskets of fruit, grain, and delicious honey cakes. The bishop collected the gifts and sailed away to the poor and hungry town. He arrived at night, and in the darkness, he crept to the first lighted house and knocked on the window. The mother inside asked her small child to see who knocked so late. When the child looked outside no one was there—at the door or at the window. But in the snow stood baskets, filled to overflowing with fruit and grain for the town.

December

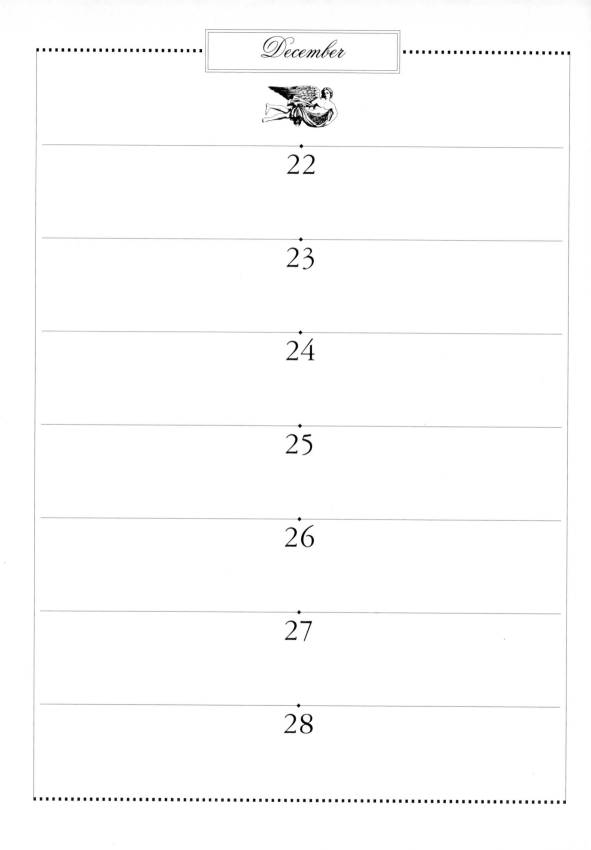

22

23

24

25

26

27

28

29

30

31

Honey-Lemon Sorbet

Ingredients

1 cup fresh lemon juice
1 cup water
⅓ to ½ cup honey, depending
   on sweetness desired
1 egg white, beaten until foamy
4 calla lilies

Method

*Combine lemon juice, water, and
honey until thoroughly blended. Stir
in egg white. Freeze in ice cream
maker as per manufacturer's instruc-
tions. Scoop onto waxed paper and
freeze until serving time. To serve,
clean the lilies with damp toweling.
Remove the central spike from
each flower. Place on serving plates
and fill with sorbet. Please note:
Calla lilies are not edible flowers.*

Yield: 4 servings.